CW00725667

Battle of S

The Prequel to the Rape of Nanking

Pacific Atrocities Education

Battle of Shanghai

*The Prequel to the
Rape of Nanking*

LUKE DIEP-NGUYEN

Battle of Shanghai

The Prequel to the
Rape of Nanking

Written by
Luke Diep-Nguyen

Editor
Barbara Halperin

Published by Pacific Atrocities Education

Paperback ISBN: 978-1-947766-31-0

E-book ISBN: 978-1-947766-20-4

Table of Contents

Chapter 1

Background

The Battle of Shanghai, during the summer of 1937, was one of the most important battles between China and Japan as it was the first major battle of the Sino-Japanese War and involved over one million troops from both sides. The battle, due to the surprisingly fierce Chinese resistance, cost Japan their sense of military and martial superiority over the Chinese. It also set the stage for Japan's desire for revenge for such a costly fight and led to one of the most horrific acts of the war, the Rape of Nanking. In order to fully understand the context behind Japan's decision to attack Shanghai and the consequent fighting, it is essential to analyze documents and articles that chronicle both the Chinese and Japanese pre-war positions and the events that finally forced the two nations to engage in one of the bloodiest and longest engagements of the Second World War.

On September 18, 1931, a Japanese-owned railway, near Mukden in Manchuria, exploded. The Japanese accused Chinese nationalists of an attempted assault on Japanese territory and used the explosion as an excuse to invade Manchuria. The untrained and under-equipped inferior Chinese force enabled the Japanese to occupy Manchuria quickly. When the invasion was carried out, the Chairman of the Chinese Nationalist Party, Chiang Kai-Shek, was more focused on the closer Communist threat[1] and hoped to use Manchuria's abundant resources to aid in its economic restoration.[2]

The need for Manchuria and its natural materials began following World War I. During the 1920s, Japan had been impacted by the global economic crash. The war's end meant decreased military needs, and munitions factory workers as well as other laborers lost their jobs. Farmers' prices for agricultural products sank and the lack of employment combined with a severely dwindling food supply resulted in widespread starvation.

---

[1] History.com Editors, "Chiang Kai-Shek," History.com (A&E Television Networks, November 9, 2009),
https://www.history.com/topics/china/chiang-kai-shek.
[2] "The Mukden Incident of 1931 and the Stimson Doctrine," U.S. Department of State (U.S. Department of State), accessed June 19, 2020,
https://history.state.gov/milestones/1921-1936/mukden-incident.

On September 1, 1923, Tokyo was struck by the 9.0 Great Kanto Earthquake, followed by a 40-foot tsunami and a fire that destroyed houses across Tokyo and Yokohama. The worst natural disaster in Japan's history not only destroyed 45% of Tokyo, but caused the deaths of 140,000 residents. The earthquake and its effect on the Japanese people provided the impetus for many militarists and imperialists to further promote patriotism. In turn, this led to both promoting Japanese expansion of colonial territory in East Asia and the onset of spreading anti-Korean propaganda about Korean immigrants poisoning wells.[3]

In 1928, Japan and its population advocated for the invasion of Manchuria and China in order to exploit their resources and territory. Following the global economic crash, Japan felt they could not rely on Western countries for economic support. That lack of trust, in turn, led to a growth in nationalist ideology. Moreover, Japanese military expansion encouraged the belief of a mentality superior to that of China and Manchuria. The Japanese believed that by conquering Manchuria, they would also be freeing it from Chinese influence, which was negatively viewed. Japan's expanding imperialist and nationalist ideology, caused by economic depression, starva-

---

[3] Joshua Hammer, "The Great Japan Earthquake of 1923," Smithsonian.com (Smithsonian Institution, May 1, 2011), https://www.smithsonianmag.com/history/the-great-japan-earthquake-of-1923-1764539/.

tion, and loss of trust in Western economic aid, became a significant factor in the need to lift Japan out of its economic crisis. It also led to feelings of superiority toward other countries, subsequently reflected in the military's treatment of their subjects, primarily the Chinese.[4]

Despite the greater concern of the communist threat, the Manchurian Incident affirmed to Chiang Kai-Shek and the Chinese people that Japan would use their conquest of Manchuria to threaten China. The Japanese aggression gave way to the rise of anti-Japanese rhetoric among the public. Chiang and the Nationalist government sought aid from the League of Nations and Western Powers, hoping that the League of Nations and countries such as the U.S., Britain, and France would pressure Japan to withdraw from Manchuria. If not, the Western powers would cease exports to Japan.[5]

The U.S. drafted a report covering both the Chinese and Japanese positions in North China. In North China in 1934, Japan implemented economically and culturally exploitative policies and strategies. Deciding to use China's Northern provinces as their base to

---

[4] Walter Zapotoczny Jr., "The Road to Nanking," Warfare History Network, December 23, 2018,
https://warfarehistorynetwork.com/2018/12/22/the-road-to-nanking/.
[5] Sun, Youli. "CHINA'S INTERNATIONAL APPROACH TO THE MANCHURIAN CRISIS, 1931-1933." *Journal of Asian History* 26, no. 1 (1992): 42-77. Accessed June 19, 2020. www.jstor.org/stable/41930841, p. 46-49.

prepare for war against the Soviet Union, Japan established and expanded transportation and communication networks across North China and Manchuria to allow faster and easier mobilization of their military in order to build up their forces in preparation for their war with the Soviet Union. In Manchuria, Japan, which had faced uprisings from the native population, faced an internal dispute between militarists and capitalists over their control of Manchuria. The structure that became the primary focus of Japan's move to exploit Manchuria was the South Manchurian Railway Company (SMR).

The SMR was essential and the main objective of the militarist and capitalist power struggle was due to conflicting positions regarding Manchuria's primary use to exploit resources for militaristic or economic purposes. While the capitalists established control over the SMR's use for political control over Manchuria, the militarists wanted control of the SMR, recognizing the importance of resources useful to prepare for possible military engagements with neighboring countries which could threaten Japan's resources in Manchuria. Both the War Ministry and General Nobuyoshi Muto, Commander in Chief of the Kwantung Army, and Governor-General of the Kwantung Leased Territory proposed that the SMR and Japan's policies over Manchuria be reorganized to tighten their economic and political hold on Manchuria and advance their economic exploitation of the nation's resources. The Kwantung Army was formed in 1919 to be dispatched to Japan's territory in Manchuria gained following the First Sino-Japanese War and Russo-Japanese War. The Kwantung Army was then the most superior army in the Pacific Asia Region. After the occupation of Manchuria in 1931, the Kwantung army established a puppet government independent from administrative control. It brought approximately a million Japanese citizens to settle in Manchuria. Through their puppet government, the Army gained political, economic and military control over the state and its newly established independent status enabled it to enact policies without interference from Tokyo.[6] The Kwantung Army acted as Japan's defense force in Manchuria and North China and funded the reorganization plan for the SMR. The entirety of the Kwantung Army's reorganization plan revolved around dissolving the established system of the SMR and forming their own, to be entirely under General Muto's complete control of its administration and operations. This plan also led to General Muto gaining full control of its executives and employees, many of whom were native Manchurians,

---

[6] Zhuoran Li, "The Role of the Kwantung Army in Japan's Relationships with China During 1920s and 1930s," Medium (Medium, February 8, 2017), https://medium.com/@ZLi/the-role-of-the-kwantung-army-in-japans-relationships-with-china-during-1920s-and-1930s-4734098a124b.

and allowing the Kwantung Army greater control of the economic and political situation in Manchuria. General Muto and many of the army staff felt the Japanese Government lacked an understanding of the importance of Japan's different position or degree of ambition required to take necessary actions for the benefit of the nation. These qualities resided with the military, which firmly believed that Japan's national economy and defense were essential in maintaining their power, thus retaining control over Manchuria.

By this time, though Manchuria gained its status as an independent state, it served as a puppet state to Japan. Unfortunately, the SMR had a significant part in controlling Manchuria's economic and political state and, under the new reorganization plan, it would be directly under General Muto. The Kwantung Army, through powerful influence, achieved full control of political and economic operations in Manchuria and severed the SMR's ties with the Ministry of Overseas Affairs, which had previously held supervision over the SMR. The abolition of the Ministry of Overseas Affairs' administration over the SMR allowed total authoritative control under the Commander-in-Chief of the Kwantung Army.[7]

---

[7] Chen Pen-ho, "Militarism vs. Capitalism for Control of Manchuria: Conflict Over SMR Reconstruction Question." INT/JMMoh-jop, Shanghai, 1934.

While the Kwantung Army was establishing their power over Manchuria and North China, General Chiang Kai-Shek, Commander-in-Chief of China's Military Affairs Commission, which ran the Nationalist Revolutionary Army, was focused on suppressing the Communists military. Chiang gathered reports and intelligence on Communist troop movements in China and Nationalist troop movements against them. When Japan's military development in Manchuria and North China escalated and political control grew, troop numbers increased China's concerns, especially since, one year earlier in 1933, Japan had resigned from the League of Nations leaving it free from adhering to the League's rules. As a result of these concerns, in March 1934, the 4th Marine Corps Expeditionary Force from Shanghai began to document Japan's economic, political, and military progress in Manchuria and North China. They observed Japan's massive increase in foreign trade expansion, agricultural and industrial production, and an increase in taxes of which nearly 45 percent of Japan's expenditures were earmarked for military funding. Taxes were used to increase agricultural production rates and fund munitions plants. There was also an increase of reinforcements from the Japanese military for garrisons in Manchuria and North China. The increase in spending on military funding and strength was a red flag for the Nationalists who were apprehensive about a possible invasion or Japanese attacks. As a result, the Nationalists began to raise their military strength near the borders between Nationalists China and Japan-occupied North China.[8]

Another indication of a possible Japanese threat to China was the increased movement of Japan's Manchukuo Navy. Their funding increased and scouting operations along the coast of China became noticeably more active. Again, in September 1935, the 4th Marines relayed information on Japan's increased funding on munitions plants and shipyards to expand the Manchukuo Navy. Since Japan opposed Communism, Chiang hoped to use that to motivate a united front with Japan against the Communists.[9] Unfortunately, the relationship between China and Japan was fragile and tense. The foreign reports were uncomfortable with such a temporary alliance since Japan's motive for acceptance was suspected to be personal gain, eliminating a possible future threat instead of wanting to aid Chiang and the Nationalist Army. At the time, Chiang was more focused on the Communists than Japan, since they seemed to be the more immediate concern.[10] By the end of the year, this view

---

[8] "Confidential Report on Conditions in Japan and Manchuria: The Forthcoming Crisis of 1935 and 1936." Shanghai, 1934.

[9] Intelligence Officer, "Navy." Manchukuo, 1935.

[10] Intelligence Officer, "Weekly Intelligence Summary for week ending 8 September 1935." Shanghai, 1935.

changed with the increase in reinforcements for the Kwantung Army and their escalation of troop movements in North China. The report tried to predict possible Japanese military escalation, including future demands to allow more troops south of the Great Wall and to increase their military power in North China.[11] The Japanese military had begun to establish and reinforce garrisons closer to the border, including a railway station near Peiping, a major city within Nationalist China. Many Chinese local settlements along the borders felt threatened by the military escalation and, therefore, raised their defenses if Japan took aggressive actions toward their positions. The Chinese military even reported on Chinese civilians, specifically in Shanghai, protesting and urging Japanese residents to petition the Japanese authorities to cease military training operations, specifically the Japanese Navy Landing Party off the coast of Shanghai. While negotiations took place between the two countries with foreign officials acting as moderators, the Japanese build-up of military power and increased Chinese troop movements toward the borders were the basis for tension that would eventually lead to war.[12]

---

[11] Ibid.

[12] Intelligence Officer, "Weekly Intelligence Summary for week ending 24 May 1936." Shanghai, 1936.

The hope for Japanese objectives for North China were to gain freedom and independence from Nationalist influence, exploit Manchuria through their economic development in North China, and promote an independent Mongolian movement to motivate an anti-Soviet movement. The increase in Japanese militarization in North China caused tension between the Japanese military and the Nationalist military, which bordered the countries.[13] On July 8, 1937, rising tensions lingering over the borders of Nationalist China and Japanese-occupied territory finally exploded into a firefight across the Marco Polo Bridge between units from the Kwantung Army and Chinese Nationalists border military. While there have been different interpretations and views on the context behind the incident, its result was unquestionable. Both countries blamed the other for the casualties that occurred as well as violations of the agreements between the two countries. Japan insisted that China apologize for their actions and punish the officers who were responsible for firing weapons and also proposed that both countries withdraw their military forces from the local border settlements. General Chiang refused to apologize for their actions or punish his officers since China believed that it was Japan who violated their agree-

---

[13] Nihon Gaiji Kyōkai, "Why Japan Had to Fight for Shanghai." The Foreign Affairs Association of Japan, Tokyo, 1937, p. 1.

ments. Instead, he sent additional troops north. He decided that, since Japan was mobilizing troops and reinforcing their North China Army, it was essential to do the same to prepare for a possible Japanese threat.

The increase in Chinese troop movements exacerbated hostilities between the two countries, particularly among their front-line units, so much so, that on the night of July 25th, General Katsuki of Japan's North China Army and General Hsiu-Ping, Vice Chief of China's Central China Army, acting on their heightened hatred and friction towards the other, they involved in several engagements with each other. The hostilities only ceased after July 27 when units on both sides were ordered to retreat. Hoping to avoid a full-scale war and solve the rising hostilities between border units, Japanese Prime Minister Fumimaro Konoe and his Cabinet reached out to Nanking to find a political solution to their problems. Throughout the beginning of August, the governments of China and Japan proposed conflicting policies and neither side was willing to compromise.

The Japanese Army General Staff and the Nationalist military hoped to encourage a diplomatic solution. However, conflict and tensions between the Nationalist Government and the Inner Cabinet of Japan perpetuated the tension and border hostilities. The Inner Cabinet with the Japanese ministers finally decided that the only solution to resolving their issues was using military force. The Japanese War Minister and the Foreign Minister proposed that the Japanese military take their army through Shanghai towards Nanking and force cooperation between the two nations.[14]

---

[14] Crowley, James B. "A Reconsideration of the Marco Polo Bridge Incident." *The Journal of Asian Studies* 22, no. 3 (1963): 277-91. https://doi.org/10.2307/2050187.

Chapter 2

Shanghai

The city's political, economic, and cultural structure provided a background for understanding the importance of Shanghai to the Japanese military and political leaders. Japan's interests in Shanghai arose due to its upcoming engagement in foreign investments and settlements.

Since the 1920s, Shanghai had been establishing itself as a center for international political, economic, and cultural exchanges. Because of their investment in international trade and settlements for foreigners, Shanghai became more significant as a global geopolitical and economic influence. Foreign presence easily promoted the increased exchange of political, economic, and cultural ideas. As Shanghai became more dependent on foreign imports and exports, industries were established to support the foreign markets. The Shanghai Power Company supplied industries with electricity to help support production. In 1934, Shanghai's popularity and increased demand for supplies led to the growing need for electricity to increase production. The Shanghai Power Company sold almost 750 million kilowatts of electricity to different industries, the most important one being the cotton industry which constituted 77.8% of the Power Company's sales between 1930 and 1934. Other industries included flour, rubber, paper, and tobacco.

Shanghai's success and influence worked two ways. It profited off of foreign traders and companies that, attracted by Shanghai's influence and success, came there to sell and buy goods. In return, the foreign market profited from their exploits in the city while also spreading news of Shanghai and its global market which benefited the city. Shanghai relied on its foreigners to contribute to its growth. Since the mid-19th century, foreigners had been attracted to the city. In 1843, botanist Robert Fortune described his experience arriving in Shanghai and his amazement at how packed the port was. Fortune's experience mirrored that of many early foreigners who were amazed at the heavy traffic within the port. Even during its early genesis as an international industrial and trading center, Shanghai had still attracted a large number of companies and industries, including the American trading house Russell and Company and the British foreign trading company Jardine Matheson and Company. The latter became one of the largest foreign trading companies of the 19th century.[15] The emergence of Sino-Japanese hostilities in the early 1930s brought a new threat to Nationalist China and their struggle with the Communist Party. The threat allowed Shanghai to expand its political and economic opportunities, including its involvement in international administration in Shanghai and its foreign trade and industrial development.[16]

During the mid-19th century, Shanghai was split into three main independently governed sections: The International Settlement, the French Concession, and Greater Shanghai. The International Settlement, overseen by the Municipal Council, was an area on the outskirts of Shanghai proper and housed foreigners. The Municipal Council consisted of nine foreign officials, including five British, two Americans, and two Japanese, along with five Chinese officials. The settlement was protected by the Shanghai Volunteer Corps, the settlement's law enforcement organization funded and supplied by both the British War Office and the American Government. The Shanghai Volunteer Corps was also seen to be mili-

---

[15] Orchard, John E. "Shanghai." *Geographical Review* 26, no. 1 (1936): 1-31. Accessed June 30, 2020. doi:10.2307/209460, p. 6-7, 26.
[16] Lockwood, William W. "The International Settlement at Shanghai, 1924-34." *The American Political Science Review* 28, no. 6 (1934): 1030-046. Accessed May 18, 2020. doi:10.2307/1947378, p. 1031.

tarily mobilized during threats such as the conflicts between the Chinese and Japanese in 1932 and the entrance of Nationalists forces in 1927. Over the years since its establishment in 1843, the foreign population the International Settlement steadily increased, which led to slow growth of the area and its community.

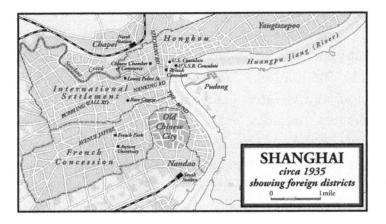

Map of Shanghai in 1935[17]

The French Concession was established in 1844 when France granted rights to settle a French community into five Chinese communities, including Shanghai, Nanking, Canton, Amoy, and Foochow. While there were Americans and British conces-

---

[17] Warfare History Network, 1935,
https://warfarehistorynetwork.com/wp-content/uploads/The-Fall-Of-Shanghai-Prelude-To-The-Rape-Of-Nanking-WWII-5.jpg.

sions, they were soon merged with the International Settlement while the French community remained independent. Following the occupation of Shanghai from Nationalists in 1926, the Greater Shanghai municipality and the city government was established. Greater Shanghai was designated as under the jurisdiction of the Nationalist Government and surrounded by foreign municipal areas which were independently administered. By the 1930s, Shanghai's population totaled 3.5 million.

In 1932, the Peace Preservation Corps was established in Shanghai as the police force. Its main objective was to maintain order in neutral areas around Shanghai and parts of Shanghai outside of the International Settlement and French Concession. The Corps initially started with a force of 5,000 but had doubled in size by 1936. Before Japan invaded Nationalist China, Japanese officials studied Shanghai to assess their situation for the purpose of developing their strategy. While the Peace Preservation Corps was meant to be the police force, it was funded and supplied by the Nationalist Army, which resulted in their equipment being the same as that of the regular Chinese troops. Upon any sign of a threat, the Peace Preservation Corps could be mobilized as a defensive military force.[18]

---

[18] Nihon Gaiji Kyōkai, "Why Japan Had to Fight for Shanghai," p. 2-8.

Following the Russo-Japanese War and rapid Japanese industrial and population growth resulting from their victory, the Japanese population on mainland Asia increased, particularly in major international cities such as Shanghai. In order to handle the task of unifying and protecting the Japanese community in Shanghai, the Japanese Ministry of Foreign Affairs passed the Resident Association Act, which helped create the Japanese Resident Association (JRA). The JRA created schools and clubs in order to form a protected close community. The Japanese presence and treatment in Shanghai strengthened the reason for the Japanese military to engage with China, particularly with Shanghai. Shanghai's presence in Japan's political and economic growth allowed Japan to witness changes made in and around the city and to examine its future potential in Japanese-held territories in North China, Manchuria, and the Japanese living in Shanghai.[19]

Shanghai was essential to Japan not only because of its political and strategic position but also because of the threat it posed to the Japanese-occupied territories of North China. A vengeful sentiment towards anti-Japanese movements occurred towards the Japanese population in the International Settlement. In

---

[19] Fogel, Joshua A. "Shanghai-Japan: The Japanese Residents' Association of Shanghai." *The Journal of Asian Studies* 59, no. 4 (2000): 927-50. Accessed May 19, 2020. doi:10.2307/2659217, p. 929-930.

1937, the Kuomintang, threatened by an increase of Japanese military strength in North China, sent more Chinese military forces to Shanghai and areas around Shanghai to build up a defensive force. Following the Marco Polo Bridge Incident, 100,000 Chinese troops from the 36th, 87th, 88th, 27th units and the 33rd Division were stationed. The Chinese force also included artillery units, engineers, and other support troops. Furthermore, the Japanese felt the Chinese Peace Preservation Corps was a military force disguised as a law enforcement organization. With the escalation of Chinese militarization in Shanghai and increasing tensions and conflicts between China and Japan, the Japanese felt their Shanghai population was threatened and, therefore, landed their Naval Landing Party with marines and naval troops to protect the Japanese nationals from potential threats from the Chinese military. Simultaneously, the Japanese government worked to evacuate Japanese nationals from the International Settlement. By August, the Japanese Army advanced in Shanghai to support the marines and beat back the Chinese military.[20]

Another factor that incentivized Japan to attack Shanghai was retaliation for anti-Japanese sentiments and movements in Shanghai. Since the Japa-

---

[20] Nihon Gaiji Kyōkai, "Why Japan Had to Fight for Shanghai," p. 13-14, 22-23.

nese invasion of Manchuria in 1931, along the Yangtze Valley, there were anti-Japanese coalitions which encouraged the boycott of Japanese goods and businesses. Anti-Japanese organizations included members of the Chinese Postal Workers Union and Chinese students. The National Federal Chinese Chambers of Commerce hoped to obstruct Japanese industrial and economic development in Shanghai. Many Chinese in cities throughout the Yangtze Valley, including Hongkew (Hongkou), Shanghai, and Nanking, organized anti-Japanese movements which advocated the imprisonment of Chinese who bought Japanese goods and were employed by or worked with Japanese businesses. Other anti-Japanese approaches included requiring registration of Japanese goods, collecting registration fees, inspecting and seizing Japanese goods, and refusing to buy, sell or transport them, along with other methods restricting Japanese profits in China. In Shanghai, between September and October of 1931, anti-Japanese organizations seized Japanese goods transported by Japanese merchants, and Japanese newspaper carriers were robbed of their deliveries. As a result, Japanese companies reduced importing goods and their contracts with individual businesses were canceled or suspended. Due to the loss of income from materials, many Japanese stores and businesses were forced to close. In addition to the economic restrictions, the Japanese were victims of Chinese anti-Japanese violence. In Shanghai, Japanese nationals, particularly children, were stoned in public by mobs alongside other acts of physical violence.[21]

As the Japanese population increased, so did anti-Japanese feelings in Shanghai. The boycotts and anti-Japanese protests in Shanghai were deemed to be in retaliation for the lack of Japanese officials to intercept anti-Chinese actions in Korea. In response to the anti-Japanese actions, the JRA, along with the Japanese Commercial League of Shanghai, worked with businesspeople to assist in appealing to the government. Assemblies were held during October 1931 to organize a united front. While Japanese business people pushed the Government to take a more proactive role in punishing China for their anti-Japanese activities, higher local Japanese officials in Shanghai, including the chairman of the JRA and the leading officials of the Residents' Council, also led actions for the protection of Japanese nationals from anti-Japanese movements. Their actions took the form of the creation of the Emergency Board, which was funded by the JRA and headed by the Japanese Consul-General in Shanghai, Murai

---

[21] Japanese Chamber of Commerce of Los Angeles. *The present situation in Manchuria and Shanghai: the reason why Japan decided to dispatch a portion of her army to Shanghai* (Los Angeles, Calif: Japanese Chamber of Commerce of Los Angeles, 1930), p. 13-14.

Urumatsu. The Board's tasks were to manage housing, food distribution, and communications within the Japanese community in the International Settlement and press the Japanese government for military support. Additionally, the JRA increased the community's contribution and responsibility by becoming involved with the local government and police agencies, forming a postal service, informing the Japanese press about the Japanese situation in Shanghai, and transforming JRA-run schools into military and medical facilities.[22]

The climax to Japan's eventual invasion of China and assault on Shanghai involved multiple factors, the most prominent one being ethnic tension and discrimination. As an international municipality and major center for international trade in China, Shanghai became an essential asset for Japan when they were planning on entering China. Shanghai established foreign settlements, which made it a key position for international trade and relations, but their economic, political, and strategic importance made it a target for threats.

---

[22] Fogel, Joshua A. "Shanghai-Japan: The Japanese Residents' Association of Shanghai." *The Journal of Asian Studies* 59, no. 4 (2000): 927-50. Accessed May 24, 2020. doi:10.2307/2659217, p. 934-936.

**WHY JAPAN HAD TO FIGHT
IN SHANGHAI**

THE FOREIGN AFFAIRS ASSOCIATION OF JAPAN

Price: 50 Sen

Japanese Booklet "Why Japan Had to Fight in Shanghai"[23]

---

[23] Nihon Gaiji Kyōkai. *Why Japan Had to Fight in Shanghai*, 1937, Foreign affairs association of Japan; Special Collections & Archives, Queen's University Belfast,
http://digital-library.qub.ac.uk/digital/collection/p15979coll28/id/4930.

Chapter 3

The First Battle of Shanghai of 1932

The battle of Shanghai in 1937 was not the only Japanese military conflict with the Chinese in that city. At the start of 1932, after years of prejudice and discrimination based tension and hostility between the two ethnic communities, the Japanese government decided to respond militarily against the discrimination that Japanese nationals faced and sent the navy and army support them. The battle involved the mass destruction of a city and a considerable number of both military and civilian casualties. The catastrophe that Shanghai faced in 1932 became a precursor to the battle between Japan and China in 1937. Both battles became indications of modern urban warfare and the mass destruction and devastation it was possible to inflict. In later years, the consequences of battles in Stalingrad, Manila, and Ortona would echo those of the two battles of Shanghai.[24] Following an attack on Japanese Buddhist priests by Chinese workers who were members of the Anti-Japanese Association, Japanese General-Consul Murai demanded an apology from the mayor of Shanghai as well as the attackers' arrest and suppression of all anti-Japanese organizations and activities in the city. While the mayor accepted and agreed to those demands, the Chinese military force in Shanghai, which consisted of the 19th Route Army and the 5th Army, was positioned in the city. The 19th Army was positioned in the Hongkew and Chapei (Zhabei) districts. Feeling threatened by that military presence, the Japanese decided to deploy a defensive naval landing based on the need for protection in the event of military action against the Japanese settlement. On January 28th, the initial skirmish took place in the Hongkew district following the arrival of the Japanese naval force. The 19th Army was also threatened by the Japanese troops as they entered the district and set up a defensive position, which ultimately led to a firefight between the two. The Japanese troops felt strongly that their involvement with the Chinese was an act of self-defense.

At the onset of the battle, only 3,000 Japanese troops faced 31,000 Chinese troops of the 19th Route Army. In an attempt to level the playing field, the Jap-

---

[24] Christian Henriot, "Beyond Glory: Civilians, Combatants, and Society During the Battle of Shanghai," *War & Society* 31, no. 2 (2012): 106-108.

anese Navy dispatched an aircraft carrier to launch an aerial assault against the Chinese positions in the Chapei district without endangering their Japanese nationals. The Japanese naval air force took the most effective measures. First, reconnaissance planes were sent to mark targets in advance of the bombers. Secondly, to ensure the accuracy of their bombing and guarantee that there would be no accidental bombing on the Japanese positions, the Japanese flew as close to the ground as permitted. Finally, targets that were marked for the most effectiveness included Chinese military positions, supply trains, and a mass gathering of Chinese troops, which seemed to be a possible position for an attack. Unfortunately, because the planes flew at a low altitude, they were vulnerable to ground fire. Following the bombing, a truce was proposed and established to provide a neutral zone in the Chapei district where peaceful Shanghai residents could be evacuated to avoid the battle. During the truce, however, the Chinese military attempted to reinforce their position which the Japanese felt was a violation of the truce. In response to the Chinese military build-up, the Japanese naval party called for reinforcements of their own, which recommenced the fighting in February.[25]

---

[25] Navy Department, *The Shanghai Incident and the Imperial Japanese Navy* (Tokyo: Navy Department, 1932), https://digitalrepository.trincoll.edu/cgi/viewcontent.cgi?article=1005&context=moore, p. 4-13.

On February 6, the Japanese 9th Division, the 24th Mixed Brigade detachment from the 12th Division, and two squadrons were formed to organize an expeditionary force to reinforce the navy force. The Japanese reinforcements landed at Shanghai between February 13 and February 16.[26] Following the arrival of the Japanese expeditionary force, Lieutenant-General Kenkichi Uyeda established around the Japanese community a safeguard against threats from the Chinese military. He met with the 19th Route Army's Chief of Staff of to propose an end to hostilities between the Japanese and Chinese and to propose that both military forces withdraw 20 km from their positions by February 20 at 7 a.m., which would ensure that the Chinese military respected the proposal. While the Japanese remained in the Japanese district of Shanghai, upon ending the conflicts, they would not take any offensive actions against the Chinese and only act as a protective force. By February 20, the Chinese had not withdrawn their military. Lt. General Uyeda felt this was an act of defiance and a rejection of the proposal. At 7:30 in the morning, after the Chinese military had been scheduled to withdraw from their position, the Japanese 9th Division took offensive action, making multiple

---

[26] Herald of Asia, *Fighting Around Shanghai* (Tokyo: The Herald Press, 1932), https://digitalrepository.trincoll.edu/cgi/viewcontent.cgi?article=1002 &context=moore, p. 1-4.

simultaneous assaults. The 9th Division and 24th Mixed Brigade pushed against the Chinese defenses at the Woosung (Wusong) and Kiangwan (Jianghan) districts at the port end. At the same time, the Japanese landing party cleared Chinese positions in Chapei, and the two groups hoped to meet in the middle and expel the Chinese military force from Shanghai. The Japanese also provided artillery and aerial support for their expeditionary force. Despite stubborn resistance at Kiangwan and Woosung, by the end of the next day, the Japanese had forced the Chinese troops to the edge of the districts. Concurrently, the Japanese Naval Landing Party had also pushed elements of the Chinese 19th Route Army out of Chapei and set up a defensive perimeter around their position.

At midnight on the 22nd, the Chinese launched a series of counterattacks under artillery support, but every single one was repelled. By the third day of fighting, the Japanese 9th Division had begun to move against Miaohang to the left of the Kiangwan district. Like the Chinese positions at Kiangwan and Woosung, Miaohung also had a strong, organized defensive position with well-prepared defenses. To create an opening in the Chinese lines, on the night of the 21st to 22nd, the Japanese dispatched engineers and explosive squads to cut the wire emplacements under cover of darkness and smoke screens. Sergeant Umada gathered three parties of three men to be led by himself to set explosives and use wire cutters to exploit the Chinese defenses. Each party sent either was killed, disabled, or driven back due to heavy firing from the Chinese positions. After his entire group was incapacitated, Sergeant Umada ran into the lines lobbing hand grenades to cause confusion, which allowed him to cut the wire emplacements. That deed allowed Japanese troops to exploit the gap and capture that sector of Miaohang.

From February 23 to 24, rather than continuing to push back the Chinese forces from their defensive positions, Japanese military leaders, who realized their forces had sustained heavy casualties despite their victories, started planning a new offensive emphasizing concentration of their units at critical positions that could be exploited as opposed to trying to hit the entire defensive line. During this time, as the Japanese moved their troops into position in preparation for the new offensive, the Chinese launched multiple counterattacks. However, they failed to make any significant dents in the Japanese line and each attack was repulsed.

On February 25, the 24th Mixed Brigade aimed their attack toward the Miaohang occupied sections while the 9th Division launched their offensive against key Chinese defenses at the Kiangwan district. To increase the effectiveness and damage of the offensive, the artillery and aerial units provided aid to the troops by bombarding the pre-marked targets. The barrage from the heavy artillery and bombers in tandem with the assaults from experienced shock troopers allowed it to successfully rout the Chinese. By the 27th, the Japanese were able to claim the Miaohang district and most of the Kiangwan district. The Chinese were forced to reform along a second line in the Tachang-chen district.

Chinese troops from the 19th Route Army[27]

Following the Japanese success, there was a lull in the battle as Japan sent reinforcements to the expeditionary force in the form of the 11th and 14th Divi-

---

[27] World War II Database, 1932,
https://ww2db.com/image.php?image_id=521.

sions, to replace heavy casualties sustained during previous offensives. The reinforcements landed on February 29 alongside General Yoshinori Shirakawa, who took over as Commander of the Expeditionary Force. At the same time, the Chinese 19th Army withdrew and reformed their defensive lines at Tachangchen and the remaining sectors between Kiangwan and Miaohang. The new line at Tachangchen was also formed by the 60th and 61st Divisions of the 19th Army.

On March 1, the Japanese 9th Division, the 24th Mixed Brigade, and three reinforced infantry battalions targeted the Chinese positions between Miaohang and Kiangwan. That same day, the 11th Division, with the assistance from the navy, landed from the Yangtze River against the Chinese garrison at Woosung. In cooperation with the naval bombardment, the 22nd Infantry Regiment of the 11th, under heavy machine-gun fire, quickly overwhelmed the fortress and linked up with the 24th Mixed Brigade. After clearing their objectives, the 9th Division continued their advances towards the new defense line at Tachangchen. The Japanese expeditionary force linked together to push against the Chinese positions at Chiencheng and Chenju along the Yangtze River. At the same time, the landing party cleared Chinese troops in Chapei, catching the Chinese military force in a pincer. Finally, by March 5, the

Chinese and Japanese ceased hostilities as the Chinese leaders, after their forces were largely depleted and defeated, succumbed to Japanese demands to withdraw to marked locations in Shanghai and agreed to stop all aggressive actions. In return, the Japanese military departed and suspended all military actions.[28]

Overall, the Chinese troops engaged in Shanghai numbered from 40,000 to 63,000, while Japanese numbers reached 47,000 after much initial resistance and hardship during the early stages of the battle. Japanese casualties included 769 killed in action and another 8,622 wounded, while the Chinese casualties reached 3,969 killed and over 7,698 wounded. The high casualty rate for the Chinese forces could be attributed to the heavy artillery shelling and bombing. While the military casualties were high and cost both sides dearly, the effect of the battle on the civilian population was staggering. Over 8,000 were killed, 2,000 wounded, and over 10,000 civilians were missing. However, the most significant impact of the battle rested with the reconstruction of the city.

The battle left the city devastated, and a majority of the civilian population was caught in the middle of the combat zones. Due to stray bombs and artillery shells, over 180,000 family homes were de-

---

[28] Herald of Asia, *Fighting Around Shanghai*, p. 11-31.

stroyed, including the entire Chapei district and 262 buildings from the International Settlement. After the battle, thousands of civilians from hospitals and military medical colleges in Shanghai arrived to rescue civilians trapped in the devastated areas and treat wounded soldiers and civilians, both Chinese and Japanese. Medical assistance in Shanghai became vital for the city's restoration. Shanghai encompassed the largest number of doctors and 7 of the 13 largest medical facilities in China. Aid also came from humanitarian and volunteer organizations such as the Red Cross, the Red Swastika Society, the People's Relief Association, and the Boy Scouts of Shanghai. The General Federation of Trade dispatched the largest number of volunteers to aid in rescuing Japanese and Chinese soldiers and civilians from the battle torn area. Approximately 10,000 volunteers provided rescue aid, 3,000 of which were members of the General Federation. Volunteers from the Boy Scouts helped rescue 2,000 civilians. In total, 75,000 civilians were pulled from the battle scarred area. The volunteers both treated the wounded and evacuated civilians from the devastated areas. Religious organizations such as Christian churches, Catholic societies, and other Christian medical colleges dispatched volunteers to provide medical assistance.

Despite their former hostility and aggression, the Japanese army dispatched their troops to aid in the city's cleanup. They worked alongside their Chinese counterpart and the Shanghai Municipal Council. Aid came in the form of rescue missions and medical assistance, as well as financial and logistical support by providing resources such as goods, money, and areas in which to set up medical facilities and housing for the refugees. Roads and bridges were also built to facilitate transportation of wounded and refugees to safe zones and make it easier to reach areas destroyed by the battle with no usable roads or river crossing. Many of the significant points of the battle from the initial aggression and its devastating impact on its repercussions and resolutions would be mirrored five years later.

Map showing key battles and Japanese and Chinese positions
during the Battle of Shanghai in 1932[29]

[29] C. Y. Soo. "Map Showing Japanese-Chinese Warfare Now in Shanghai."
"Norman B. Leventhal Map Center". 1932.
https://www.flickr.com/photos/normanbleventhalmapcenter/2674774585/.

Chapter 4

Battle of Shanghai, 1937

Chiang Kai-Shek, expecting the inevitable threat to Shanghai, deployed the 87th and 88th Divisions to defend the city due to its economic value as an international city and its close proximity to the Chinese capital, Nanking. The Chinese Nationalist Army had 1.5 million troops, but the quality ranged widely. The 87th and 88th made up 80,000 troops known as the "Generalissimo's Own" were better equipped, more experienced and, most importantly, better trained than any other units of the Nationalist Army. They were outfitted by foreign, mostly German, equipment, and trained by German advisers, General Hans Von Seekt and General Alexander von Falkenhausen, veterans of the First World War. While still considered inferior to the Japanese Imperial Army, by the Nationalist Army's standards, they were elite quality and had the potential to outperform above their weight class. While their helmets and design for their small arms weapons were adopted from the Germans, their tanks and machine guns were of other European models. The defense of Shanghai consisted of three tank battalions: the Polish FT-7, French Renaults, Italian CV.33, British Model 1931 amphibious tanks, and the German Panzer Mark 1A. Convinced that Chinese were training and equipment were inferior, the Japanese believed that the battle would have results similar to those of 1932, rough with some casualties, but finishing within a few days. Instead, it would take three months before the Chinese defenders submitted to the Japanese.[30]

On August 9, 1937, Sub-Lieutenant Isao Oyama of the Japanese Naval Special Forces arrived at Hongqiao Airport in Shanghai, which was against the 1932 ceasefire agreement. He was confronted by the police at the airport and killed. After the incident, the Japanese consul-general and other Japanese representatives appeared to apologize for Oyama's death and tried to convince the commander of the defense of Shanghai, General Zhang Zhizhong, and Chinese representatives to disarm the Peace Preservation Corps. Both the general and the representatives refused. General Zhang Zhizhong was

---

[30] Eric Niderost, "General Chiang Kai-Shek And Kuomintang Resisted Mao And Japanese." Warfare History Network, August 14, 2015. https://warfarehistorynetwork.com/2015/08/17/general-chiang-kai-shek-and-kuomintang-resisted-mao-and-japanese/.

already predicting the attack to come soon. This request was only another signal that Shanghai was going to become a target for the Japanese military. General Zhang was encouraged to request that Chiang send the 87th and 88th.

On the morning of August 13, 10,000 Japanese troops launched their attacks against Shanghai. The Japanese engaged with the Chinese at the Chapei, Woosung, and Kiangwan districts. The 88th was able to hold them back with mortars and artillery. At 1600, the Japanese 3rd Fleet docked along the Yangtze, and Huangu Rivers began bombarding the city as this tactic had worked well in disabling Chinese defenses in 1932 and allowed for a quick victory. This time the Chinese dispatched aircraft from Captain Gao Zhi-hang's 4th Flying Group. The bombers provided aerial support against ground movements, while the fighter planes engaged with Japanese bombers and fighters coming from Taiwan. By the end of the battle, the Chinese Air Force had shot down 85 aircraft and had sunk 51 ships while, in return, they lost 91 of their own. With the bombing of Shanghai and the aerial combat, like the battle of Shanghai, the city's infrastructure was destroyed and thousands of civilians died. Zhang, attempting to break the stalemate, launched a counterattack on August 16 by secretly closing the lines between the two positions, sneaking troops into Japanese-held buildings, and engaging in close combat fighting to overwhelm them and retake the positions. These were successful, goal accomplishing tactics successfully used by the Soviets in Stalingrad. First, it prevented naval and aerial support from targeting Chinese positions in fear of hitting their own. Second, the Chinese troops were able to surprise and overtake the Japanese troops with grenades and torches to flush out the Japanese from the buildings and shoot any stragglers with machine gunfire. The next day, the Japanese deployed their light tanks to counterattack the Chinese advances. While the Chinese were able to push back the Japanese initial advances, they could not penetrate the Japanese lines or make much progress. Chiang, feeling that Zhang failed to make any significant breakthroughs, decided to take control of and responsibility for the battle. The Chinese 36th Division arrived on August 18 at Huishan to reinforce the 87th and coordinate a tank-infantry counterattack. The attack aimed to break and penetrate the Japanese and continue the pressure to prevent further counterattacks. Unfortunately, the Chinese lacked tank-infantry coordination and their attack failed with the loss of 90 officers and 1,000 men.

The Japanese, on the other hand, dispatched their reinforcements. General Iwane Matsui, with the assistance of naval support, reinforced their Shanghai forces using the 3rd, 8th, and 11th Divisions. The three divisions landed north of Shanghai in the towns of

Chuanshakou, Shizilin, and Baoshan. Their objective was to draw Chinese troops away from the city to release pressure from the Japanese troops in the city and pull the Chinese force into a meat grinder. The Chinese troops, which arrived in an attempt to block the landings, were defeated by the reinforcements with support of naval bombardment. At Woosung, another landing of Japanese troops took place, where Chinese troops, again, attempted to counter them but failed due to the naval support. By the end, the Japanese were able to overtake Baoshan and wipe out the 98th Division, where only one Chinese survived. After the Chinese failure to prevent Japanese reinforcements and suffering heavy casualties, Chiang believed that the army needed to reform and preserve their force. He decided to go on the defensive and hold on to the territories they still had and looked to the U.S. with hope of support. Unfortunately, the U.S., afraid of being dragged into another foreign conflict, would not send troops.[31] While the U.S. could not physically support their ally, they could send weapons and supplies to Shanghai. U.S. -built Northrop 2E attack aircraft were added to the Chinese Air Force, and the U.S. allowed the Chinese to use the U.S.S. Augusta to aid

---

[31] Peter C. Chen. "Second Battle of Shanghai." WW2DB. https://ww2db.com/battle_spec.php?battle_id=85.

in their naval support.[32]

During the beginning of September, the Chinese added four more divisions to their strength, bringing their defense force to fifteen divisions. General Zhang had also moved another 50,000 Chinese troops into the Shanghai area. General von Falkenhausen advised settling 300,000 troops in the town of Luodian, which was strategically important as a transportation center. On September 11, in coordination with tanks and artillery, aerial, and naval support, 100,000 Japanese troops entered the city to take the town. Though the battle only lasted a few days, it cost both sides heavy casualties. Despite being under intense bombardment, the Chinese held firmly and were able to hold back the Japanese force. Only following aerial, artillery, and naval bombardments were Japanese able to advance against the disorientated and softened defenses. Although they courageously held back the Japanese against odds, after suffering 50% casualties, the Chinese troops were forced to evacuate from the town on September 15.

From Luodian, the Japanese troops decided to move on Dachang which was essential to both the Chinese and the Japanese for a few reasons. First, it

---

[32] Carl Gnam. "The Fall Of Shanghai: Prelude To The Rape Of Nanking & WWII." Warfare History Network, February 27, 2020. https://warfarehistorynetwork.com/2015/08/17/the-fall-of-shanghai-prelude-to-the-rape-of-nanking-wwii/.

was the communication hub for the Chinese Army. Secondly, it protected Shanghai's flank. Its loss would cost the Chinese a comprehensive means to communicate with outside forces and request more support, but it would also expose the sides of the Chinese Army and force them deeper into Shanghai. Unlike Luodian, Dachang was more fiercely defended and made deadly assaults against Japanese positions, defended by machine guns and artillery. The battle quickly became a war of attrition with little ground gained at the cost of heavy casualties. While the Chinese had been able to hold on, they relied on their reinforcements for a breakthrough. On October 17, reinforcements arrived in the form of the Guanxi Army with whom the Chinese defenders coordinated a counterattack. Unfortunately, it was poorly coordinated and failed with substantial consequences, leaving the Chinese force unable to defend the city effectively and forced to retreat on October 25.[33]

By this time, it did not seem that the Chinese would survive for much longer. They were now surrounded by 300,000 Japanese troops. Their casualty rate was detrimental—the Chinese lost ten for every one Japanese loss. During counterattack offensives, the casualty rate rose to 1,000 men dying every hour. Despite the staggering losses the Chinese Army suf-

---

[33] Peter C. Chen. "Second Battle of Shanghai."

fered, they still were willing to gather their remaining forces and make the Japanese pay for every life they lost. After the fall of Dachang, the Chinese Army was forced south of the Suzhou Creek. To fall back into a better-defended position, the Chinese Army had to give up the Chapei district. Constant bombing and shelling had left the entire district in ruins, resembling a moonscape with shell craters and bare remains of buildings. The air above Shanghai smelled of decomposing corpses and ashes.

Chiang had decided the decimated 88th be pulled into the reserve, but left a single regiment, the 524th, under Lt. Colonel Xie Jinyuan, at the North Railway Station and Sihang Warehouse at the northern end of the Suzhou Creek. The 524th would face the brunt of the oncoming Japanese attackers. The warehouse would later be known as the "Chinese Alamo" for the ferocious fighting that occurred to hold off the attack long enough for the remaining Chinese Army to reform and prepare their new defensive position. The Japanese began their attack on the warehouse on October 27. To match elements of the elite 88th, the Japanese sent one of their elite divisions, the 3rd Division. They attempted to outflank the building but were pelted by grenades and machine gun fire from the roof and upper floors of the warehouse. Before retreating, 20 Japanese troops were killed with an uncounted number wounded, but they were able to set fire to the northwest corner of the building and force the Chinese defenders out of that area. That night, the Chinese troops were able to extinguish the fire and refortify the position. The Chinese had lost two men and four were wounded. The 3rd Division was supported by mortars, artillery, tanks, the form of Type 94 Te-ke tankette, and the Japanese Air Force.

October 28 began with Japanese bombers beginning their pass over the warehouse but were unable to make any effective bombing runs since the warehouse was too close to the International Settlement. Any bombs that missed the warehouse could accidentally hit a building within the settlement that housed Western occupants, which could cause an international incident. At 8:00 in the morning, Xie and his men spotted Japanese attempting to outflank them along the Suzhou Creek. The Chinese defenders immediately opened up on the Japanese troops. While the Chinese defenders were occupied with the Japanese troops at the creek, the Japanese occupied the Bank of Communications, west of the warehouse, and used that building as the jumping-off point for their assault. The Chinese recovered and fired on the Japanese attackers with rifles and machine guns. After two hours of bitter fighting, the Japanese unit had broken off from their attack but managed to cut off the Chinese's water and electricity. The Japanese surrounded the warehouse from three sides but were unable to get around to the side facing the creek as it faced the British part of the International Settlement. The British soldiers threatened to fire on any Japanese trying to cross that way.

By the evening of October 28, impressed with their ability and the courage of the 524th, the Japanese gave the Chinese a way to surrender or be annihilated. Xie radioed the commander of the 88th, General Sun Yuanling, of the ultimatum and told Sun, "Death is an unimportant question. The sacrifice of our lives will not be in vain." The battle lasted three more days. The defenders were always under heavy artillery barrages, followed by waves of Japanese troops. At midnight on October 31-November 1, 376 Chinese troops, out of ammunition, food, and water, were evacuated across the creek to the British territory but were not allowed to return to their original division and had to "surrender" to the British for immunity. In order to be allowed to cross the creek into British territory, the Chinese defenders had to leave their weapons and be listed as refugees. The remaining Chinese, who were forced to stay, due to pressure from Japanese machine guns and artillery striking the defenders before they reached the creek, were forced to surrender, and brought to the Municipal Council.

The battle for the Sihang Warehouse and a small force of just over 400 men able to hold off against a better trained and better-equipped unit that was fifty times their size became a propaganda tool for the public opinion of China and the Chinese military in the hopes of gaining more Western support. The news press dubbed the 524th as the "Lost Battalion." From the safety of the neutral zone in the International Settlement, many Chinese civilians watched the battle for the Sihang Warehouse. They cheered when they saw the defenders push back and resist the overwhelming Japanese onslaught. Unfortunately, this would be the last major conflict in Shanghai. On November 5, the Japanese landed the 10th Army at Jinshanwei. Shanghai was now surrounded on three sides, and the Japanese were closing in fast. Chiang, wanting to spare the lives of his remaining troops, decided to evacuate the city. The evacuation started on the 8th and, by the 12th, all Chinese troops had abandoned Shanghai. However, it took until December 3rd for Shanghai to be entirely in Japanese hands, and any stragglers eliminated.[34]

During the Battle of Shanghai, at least 70,000 foreign residents were residing in Shanghai. Despite liv-

---

[34] Eric Niderost. "Chinese Alamo: Last Stand at Sihang Warehouse." Warfare History Network, October 13, 2016.
https://warfarehistorynetwork.com/2016/10/11/chinese-alamo-last-stand-at-sihang-warehouse/.

ing in the International Settlement and French Concession safety area, many of them were not left untouched by the battle surrounding them. When the Japanese bombed Shanghai on August 14, Carl Crow and Henry John May were blown on their backs from the force of the bombs that fell far from where they were. While they sustained no significant injuries, many others were not so fortunate. The bomb that fell not far from where May was worked killed Chinese refugees. British missionary editor for *The Chinese Reporter*, Frank Rawlinson, was killed by Japanese machine guns. A bomb that dropped in central Shanghai hit an elevator in a department store and killed 9 of the 11 occupants. The survivors, Anthony Billingham and a 12-year old boy were mortally wounded. Alongside regular residents involuntarily involved in the battle, some foreign journalists attempted to capture and report on it. Randall Gould snapped a photo of the Japanese battleship, *Idzumo*, shelling Chapei and Pudong's districts. A reporter of the Agence France Presse, Robert Guillain, witnessed the "surrendering" of Chinese soldiers to the French in the French Concession to escape the Japanese onslaught. They disarmed themselves and removed their helmets as they crossed into the French Concession.[35] Foreign residents, while supposed to be safe from the

---

[35] Paul French, "Too Hot—China Fights for Its Life," in Through the Looking Glass (Hong Kong: Hong Kong University Press, 2009), 195-197.

war due to their different status and residing in supposedly safe zones, were deeply affected by not only the war and battle but also by the occupation of Shanghai, as many saved Chinese refugees fleeing the battlegrounds and aided them in evacuating and setting up camps to house them. The foreign residents and reporters who documented the battle were able to quickly spread news of the battle to the Western nations.

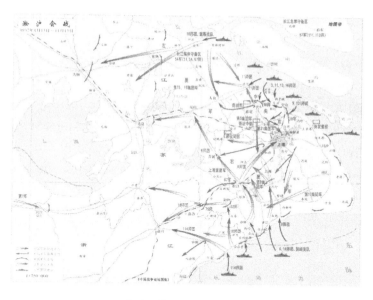

Battle of Shanghai 1937 Map[36]

---

[36] "Battle of Shanghai from August 13, 1937 to November 13, 1937" Map. 1:750,000. "Map Emperor". January 6, 2018.
http://www.dtdmap.com/china-history/minguo/1421.html.

Of the 300,000 Japanese that participated in the battle, there were 40,000 casualties. The battle cost the Chinese 250,000 of 700,000. A large number of the Chinese casualties were the German trained elite troops and their experienced leaders. The loss of over 30 percent of their force, mainly their well-trained and experienced troops, would affect their ability to fight against the Japanese in future campaigns, specifically at Nanking. The stubborn resistance of the Chinese Army showed the world, particularly Western countries, and Japan, the capability of the Chinese Army when backed against a wall. This showed that they hoped to get Japan to cease their advances, to avoid the casualties that they suffered during the battle, and to get Western countries more on their side to fight against the Japanese. While the battle of Shanghai was strategically crucial to the Sino-Japanese War, the battle's lasting impact significantly shaped the future of Shanghai and Japanese actions in China, politically and socially.

Chapter 5

Aftermath

One of the most substantial consequences of the battle was the effect on civilians, particularly the population movement. During the battle, Shanghai was bombed continuously and shelled by Chinese and Japanese bombers, artillery, and naval warships. As a result, the Chinese population was forced to flee from their homes into the International Settlement and French Concession for safety and protection from the war. While the French Concession authorities initially refused to accept refugees, the massive influx of fleeing civilians were able to escape and hide in the settlement. Many authorities and French citizens allowed fleeing them access to the concession out of humanitarian concern. In late October 1937, French authorities relaxed restrictions on refugee entry. Over a million civilians became refugees and fled to the international territories. From there, by December 1937, 375,000 had been evacuated from Shanghai. Because of the lack of resources, almost 700,000 refugees were forced to rely on friends, family, and outside support for housing, food, and medical assistance. There were over 180,000 refugees per square mile, which led to rationing food, and sharing beds, clothes, and income. While many refugees had familial support, others were not so fortunate and found themselves in dire straits—homeless and living on the streets, in abandoned buildings or on vacant lots.

Theatres became a new living site for many refugees as they squeezed together. Relief organizations were formed to provide financial, medical, and evacuation assistance. The Red Cross funded refugee assistance until early 1938 when they dropped their support and transferred their tasks to local committees. These committees included the Shanghai International Relief Committee, the Federal of Shanghai Charity Organization, and the Refugees Relief Committee. The Shanghai International Red Cross was involved in collecting funds and supplies for refugees through foreign sources. These organizations assisted in creating refugee camps. The highest number of camps established was in December 1938, with 158 camps housing 95,000 refugees.

The largest camp was the Jacquinot Safety Zone, operating on November 9, 1938, which housed approximately 250,000 refugees throughout the Japanese occupation. Due to the desperate need for medical, housing, and food funding, authorities within the International Settlement dismantled poorly equipped camps and used the resources to support well-equipped ones. Medical efforts focused on providing more vaccinations to help prevent diseases, such as cholera and smallpox. Although the refugees that lived there were mostly family, many individuals were without family members, including children. In August 1938, there were up to 1500 orphans in the International Settlement, many of whom were either separated from their families or had been deserted. Nine camps devoted themselves to building orphanages and nurseries for abandoned or separated children and babies.[37]

While the majority of refugees were Chinese natives, there was a large number of non-Chinese refugees in Shanghai. In 1938, Jewish refugees from Germany and Central Europe escaped religious persecution by fleeing to Shanghai. No strange place for them, there were already around 50,000 Russian Jews who escaped persecution from the Bolshevik Revolution in 1917. The Russian Jews accepted and aided the new Jewish refugees in settling into the International Settlement, mostly in the Hongkew district which had been destroyed by intense bombing and shelling. Upon arriving in Shanghai, the refugees established tem-

---

[37] Henriot Christian. "Shanghai and the Experience of War: The Fate of Refugees." *European Journal of East Asian Studies* 5, no. 2 (2006): 215-45. www.jstor.org/stable/23615676, 215-230.

porary refugee camps in Hongkew and used money to rebuild the districts and establish hospitals and kitchens. While the Jewish refugees no longer faced religious or racial prejudice, they experienced economic struggles and poor living standards. They gained no support from the Japanese and the Chinese Government viewed them as enemy nationals. This meant that they could not engage in trade or professions, exacerbating the inability to obtain help with food and medical assistance. In 1939, the American Jewish Joint Distribution Committee (JDC) and the United Nations Relief and Rehabilitation Administration (UNRRA) began funding the Jewish community which relied on the relief funds provided by the two organizations. They had to build kitchens, housing, and medical and educational facilities. The kitchens had to prepare food to feed 12,000 refugees, and obtaining supplies from outside sources without aid from the Japanese or Chinese government proved a daunting challenge. The JDC sent representatives to speak with the Japanese about allowing aid in the form of food and money to be brought to the Jewish community. The Japanese agreed to the requests if the Jewish community would repay the loans after the war.[38] The JDC worked with the community and with

---

[38] Laura L. Margolis, "Race Against Time in Shanghai," *Survey Graphic* 33 no. 3 (1944):168-191, https://archives.jdc.org/wp-content/uploads/2018/06/shanghai_race-against-time-in-shanghai.pdf, p. 168-171.

UNRRA for aid and support. In 1942, the JDC began sending clothes and medicine into the Hongkew ghettos and a system was created with local committees to build a hospital with European nurses and doctors that provided the community with emergency relief.[39]

One German Jew who escaped to Shanghai was Betty Grebenschikoff. In 1939, after facing persecution from his neighbors, Grebenschikoff's father brought his family, including Betty, her older sister, her mother, her aunt, and uncle, to Shanghai through a connection with a Japanese shipping company. Betty's family first transferred to Naples, Italy, from which they traveled on the *Kashima Maru* through the Suez Canal to Bombay, Hong Kong and, finally, Shanghai. Grebenschikoff and her family arrived in the Honkew district, which had been slowly repaired from the devastation of the earlier battle. The new building where Grebenschikoff settled was tight and had a community bathroom for everyone in the building. Grebenschikoff and her family were accepted and welcomed by the other residents.

The Jewish community in Hongkew was assisted by the International Refugee Organization and the

---

[39] M. A. Leavitt, "JDC Representatives in Shanghai Tells How 15,000 Refugees Survive Japanese Ghetto" (letter, Joint Distribution Committee, 1946), https://archives.jdc.org/wp-content/uploads/2018/06/shanghai_jdc-representative-in-shanghai-tells.pdf, p. 1-3, https://archives.jdc.org/wp-content/uploads/2018/06/shanghai_race-against-time-in-shanghai.pdf.

Organization of Rehabilitation and Training. While in Shanghai, Grebenschikoff and her sister went to the Shanghai Jewish School, which functioned under the auspices of the Shanghai Jewish Youth Organization. Each classroom held forty to fifty students, all of whom were taught English since all of their teachers were English. While the Jewish community was segregated, it was under Japanese jurisdiction. Specifically, the Hongkew district was under a Japanese commander known by Betty as "Mr. Goya." Each child was required to have a special pass in order to attend school. During the war, Americans continually bombed Shanghai since it was an essential port for Japan's transfer of supplies and reinforcements throughout their Empire. Betty shared that, while American bombers were gladly welcomed by Chinese and Jewish residents due to their assault on Japanese industries and the port, nearing the end of the war, bombs began dropping within the city. Many hit Hongkew and the residential area of the Jewish community, which forced the residents to be more alert and fearful of air raid sirens.[40]

Throughout the war, the JDC had granted the Jewish community $100,000 monthly. The kitchen fund provided the refugees with one daily meal of stew with vegetables and meat. Funds also were used

---

[40] June Behrens, interview by Betty Grebenschikoff, *United States Holocaust Memorial Museum*, March 10, 1990.

to help build hospitals, schools, workshops, and a theatre. After the war, in late 1945, the JDC was able to increase the monthly funding grant to $130,000 and the UNRRA joined in to provide food, medical assistance, and rent aid. The JDC also provided medical aid in the form of shipping penicillin, insulin, and other drugs for the refugees. The end of the war allowed the U.S. to send their military into Shanghai and, with the assistance of the JDC and UNRRA, they employed refugees for work such as truck drivers, clerks, and stenographers. The JDC funded emigration and migration programs that helped the Jewish refugees immigrate to the U.S., Australia, and Palestine. American Jewish soldiers, some of whom married Jewish women, helped adopt Jewish families and they and their families were assisted in returning to the U.S.[41]

A different consequence had a more significant impact on the Japanese military and, in turn, affected their treatment of the Chinese population, which led to one of the most horrific tragedies of the war. While the Japanese military always taught their soldiers honor and chivalry, what followed the Shanghai battle was anything but honorable or chivalrous.

---

[41] Raphael Levy, "12,000 Refugees in Shanghai Depend on JDC, UNRRA Aid, Jewish Army Chaplain Reports" (letter, Joint Distribution Committee, 1946), https://archives.jdc.org/wp-content/uploads/2018/06/shanghai_twelve-thousand-refugees-in-shanghai.pdf, p. 1-3.

Many factors led to the brutality committed against the Chinese population and other Japanese subjects during the war. One of the reasons was the harsh discipline and mentality ingrained in the soldiers during training. Because the Japanese military wanted hardened and loyal soldiers, they subjected recruits to harsh punishments for lack of obedience and to rigid endurance training. From early childhood, Japanese children were taught to work for the benefit of their family, community, and country and to discard selfish needs.

Jewish refugees attend a communal seder in Shanghai.[42]

---

[42] Courtesy of Alfred Brosan. *Jewish Life in Shanghai*, 1938, photograph, United States Holocaust Memorial Museum, https://collections.ushmm.org/search/catalog/pa1146106.

While these values can be beneficial and favorable to a community, they can be dangerous through a particular understanding. For example, in the Japanese military, soldiers were taught that raping victims, mostly the population of the occupied country, would make them stronger and, therefore, of greater benefit to their country and emperor. The harsh behavior of Japanese officers towards their subordinates and the similar treatment of recruits during training was reflected in the soldiers' treatment of the civilian population. Japanese soldiers believed that behavior would make them stronger and demonstrate the superiority of their military. Japanese, starting in primary schools, were also taught that they were racially superior and to hate the Chinese. Schools for Japanese boys prepared them for the military and contained war propaganda spreading the idea that the Chinese were inferior and inadequate, needed to be subjugated, and that it was morally acceptable to brutalize and kill them. Anti-Chinese rhetoric was spread by teachers, politicians, and journalists. The atrocities in Nanking were permitted and justified by the Japanese military because, to the Japanese, the Chinese were seen as animals.[43]

During the Japanese Nanking campaign, the Japanese newspaper, *Osaka Mainichi Shimbun*, published

---

[43] Walter Zapotoczny Jr., "The Road to Nanking."

an article titled, "Contest to Kill 100 People Using a Sword." The article covered two Japanese officers, Tsuyoshi Noda, and Toshiaki Mukai, who engaged in a contest to determine who could be the first to chop off 100 Chinese heads. In the newspaper, the two Japanese officers bragged about their abilities and their killing. While the acts committed by the Japanese soldiers were horrific and despicable, it is important to note the manner in which these acts were portrayed to the public, reflecting how Japanese society at the time viewed those war crimes and non-Japanese Asians, mainly Chinese. One of the article's headlines stated, "It's 89-78 in the 'Contest to Cut Down a Hundred Chinese Race.' How Heroic!" The positive and glorious portrayal of Japanese brutality demonstrated that the Japanese public approved the brutal treatment of people they felt were inferior and showed that the Japanese military could commit such actions without repercussions from their superiors or the public.[44]

In an interview with a Japanese soldier, Yasutada Nanba, a Japanese veteran of the Sino-Japanese, discussed the brutality and atrocities he was ordered to inflict on the Chinese. Yasutada described an incident on December 1, 1943, when his officer ordered a vil-

---

[44] Wyatt Redd, "The Gruesome Contest Between Two Soldiers Trying To Kill 100 With Their Samurai Swords," All That's Interesting (All That's Interesting, January 16, 2018),
https://allthatsinteresting.com/japanese-contest-to-kill-100.

lage be burned down. After sacking and pillaging the village and taking what they wanted, Yasutada and his fellow soldiers trapped villagers in their homes and set the buildings on fire. Like many Japanese, Yasutada was influenced by his training in Japan. Koichi Okawara's interview reflects more deeply this mindset and its effect on Japanese personnel. He described his experience under military training and how, during killing training, he explicitly practiced killing Chinese. On November 24, 1943, wanting to occupy a farmhouse, he killed the farmer. Like his superiors who trained him, he ordered his subordinates to do the same to the Chinese villages. Both Yasutada and Koichi, along with many other Japanese veterans, acknowledged their training, but also the part their upbringing played in introducing nationalist and patriotic ideas that intertwined with racism and aggression. While they understood they could never reconcile their actions, it was important to the Japanese veterans to raise awareness of the truth and criticize the government for their part in both encouraging and promoting their actions and also attempting to cover them up.[45, 46]

---

[45] "Aggressors' Remorse: Yasutada Nanba," CNCNEWS, accessed June 22, 2020, http://en.cncnews.cn/news/v_show/43140_Aggressors__remorse:_Yasutada_Nanba.shtml.

[46] "Aggressors' Remorse: Koichi Okawara," CNCNEWS, accessed June 22, 2020, http://en.cncnews.cn/news/v_show/43213_Aggressors__remorse:_Koichi_Okawara.shtml.

While the anti-Chinese, nationalistic, and aggressive attitudes taught Japanese to hate Chinese and normalized treating them brutally, it was the battle of Shanghai that arguably prompted the acts of brutality and atrocities on the road to Nanking and in Nanking itself. The Japanese had expected to clear Shanghai in a few days and be in Nanking in three months. Instead, the elite Chinese divisions fought the Japanese to a standstill and inflicted heavy casualties on them. The Chinese military destroyed the Japanese erroneous perception of military superiority and Chinese inferiority. As a result, the Japanese soldiers, who lost many friends to the Chinese, developed a bitter feeling of resentment. In the case of the 100-kill contest and the Rape of Nanking, Japanese soldiers, with their anti-Chinese sentiment and resentment of the Chinese damage inflicted on the Japanese soldiers, retaliated with abhorrent results. While proving the strength behind the Chinese military and shattering the belief of Japanese superiority, the battle of Shanghai led to one of the most horrific tragedies in history.[47]

---

[47] Walter Zapotoczny Jr., "The Road to Nanking."

ALSO BY LUKE DIEP-NGUYEN

LUKE DIEP-NGUYEN

TAIWAN
THE ISRAEL OF THE EAST

How China, Japan, and the United States
Influenced the Forming of a New Nation

OTHER RELATED BOOKS

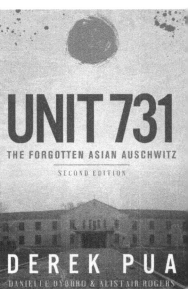

OTHER RELATED BOOKS

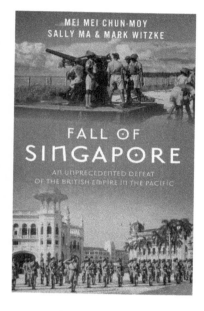

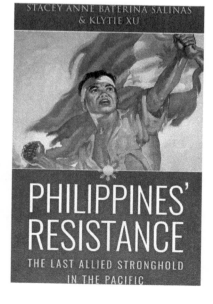